High Impact Meetings:
A Guide for Greater Productivity

Dr. Todd Thomas

For more information about this author, visit
www.drtoddthomas.com

© 2012 Impact Publications   All rights reserved. No reproduction allowed except by express written consent of the

Table of Contents

INTRODUCTION	4
HIGH-IMPACT MEETINGS	8
FORMING AN AGENDA	14
BEFORE THE MEETING BEGINS	24
OFFSITE MEETINGS	31
DURING THE MEETING	35
CLOSING AND FOLLOWING UP	40
NOW, STOP WASTING YOUR TIME!!	44
MEETING CHECKLIST	45

INTRODUCTION

"Meetings are indispensable when you don't want to do anything."
John Kenneth Galbraith

This is a short book. It was intended to be a short book. Who in their right mind would want to read a *long* book about meetings!! Unless of course you are in a meeting right now, reading this book to take your mind off the pain of sitting here. If that's what you're doing, there's plenty of white space included so you can illustrate (a.k.a. doodle) this book on your own.

What you do need however is a *short* book on meetings that has a long-term effect on both your effectiveness and your morale. If you and your colleagues can agree on nothing else, you will probably be unanimous in your feelings about meetings. There is hardly any other organizational function that brings about more frustration and personal agony than looking at a calendar and seeing that there is a meeting on the schedule. It gets even worse if there are multiple meetings which, of course, there almost always are.

While this is the type of meeting with which many of us are familiar, high-impact meetings can be an amazing tool for greater efficiency, effectiveness and satisfaction. The opportunity to have all of the decision-makers at the table or to benefit from the different perspectives in a brainstorming session can produce tremendous results.

The following tips are designed to help you turn your meetings from unproductive and annoying time-wasters to truly successful and exciting (yes, exciting!) communication opportunities. If 46 different ideas to improve your meetings are intimidating, remember that you do not have to implement all the tips included in this booklet. You should identify those tips that have the greatest potential impact and implement those first.

Try just a few of these suggestions and you will see immediate improvement in the satisfaction of participants and the overall outcome of your meetings.

So, how have you been doing so far with the meetings in which you participate? Here's a chance to find out. On the following pages, answer each question as it pertains to most of your meetings. Each item relates to a dimension of meeting effectiveness that is sometimes challenging to attain. Each item is also related to one of the tips later in the book.

1. If there is no agenda a day before the meeting, the meeting is cancelled.	Yes / No
2. When a person attends our meetings, they are clear on why they are there and the role that they have in the discussion.	Yes / No
3. Our meetings have a limited number of items on the agenda so we have the opportunity to fully discuss the topics we cover.	Yes / No
4. The information we share at our meetings is relevant to everybody in attendance.	Yes / No
5. Our problem-solving and decision-making meetings always include participants with the right background of expertise and experience.	Yes / No
6. If our meeting is to solve a problem, all participants have a mutual interest in the solution and will benefit from the discussion.	Yes / No
7. All participants know how to get an item on the agenda.	Yes / No
8. "Review of meeting" is an agenda item at the end of every meeting.	Yes / No
9. Each meeting participant has a final copy of the agenda 24 hours in advance.	Yes / No
10. Information for discussion in our meetings is often provided as pre-work to our participants.	Yes / No
11. We start the meetings in a manner that establishes the desired tone and atmosphere for the rest of the discussion.	Yes / No
12. All participants must agree with additions and with the resulting changes to the rest of the schedule.	Yes / No
13. We use a "parking lot" to capture items that are important enough to remember but not relevant to the current meeting or discussion	Yes / No

If you find yourself answering "No" to a lot of these questions, you will unquestionably see improved results in your meetings by implementing a few of these ideas. If you answered "Yes" to most of these items, congratulations. First, you should get the feedback of the rest of your team to see if they agree with your assessment. Second, you should spend some time thinking about how you plan to keep your meetings satisfying in the future. Effectiveness never stays the same. It only gets better or it gets worse. Make sure your meetings are on track from the very beginning.

HIGH-IMPACT MEETINGS
"Our meetings are held to discuss many problems which would never arise if we held fewer meetings" Ashleigh Brilliant

1) All participants should be informed on the purpose of the meeting and why they are there.

Often, the participants of a meeting are unclear as to why there is a meeting and unsure as to why they were asked to attend. A quick call or email telling somebody you would like them to attend is not enough for them to prepare to be productive.

Meetings run much more efficiently when the attendees have the opportunity to reflect on the topics and get the right information together to fully participate. An agenda distributed to each person at least 24 hours in advance of a meeting, as well as a clear explanation of the expectations for participation will not only cut useless time out of your meeting, but will ensure it is more effective.

2) Standing meetings should be canceled if there is no clear agenda within 24 hours of the meeting.

No meeting should be held for the sake of the tradition of the meeting. Many times, teams establish a "weekly" meeting format to ensure that everybody has an opportunity to communicate to one another. These standing meetings become quickly frustrating and useless when they meet with no purpose.

The meetings that you *do* have will be more effective if you are willing to cancel meetings that are for no purpose. The people who insist that the standing meeting must happen regardless of agenda are people who have no friends. Suggest that they take the time that was usually allocated to the meeting this week and go to a bookstore or supermarket to try to make some new friends.

3) Meetings to generate ideas should have few topics and plenty of time.

In a meeting where brainstorming or considering options is important, it is crucial that enough time be allowed to truly consider the alternatives. Most meetings have far too many topics to allow the kind of discussion necessary to form new ideas and direction. By allowing more time for this activity, effort is saved in re-examining topics and considering further options in later meetings.

Similar to Tip #2, this means that some of the trusted and comfortable agenda items may have to be moved during a brainstorming meeting in order to allow the flexibility to be creative. If you take a few minutes at the beginning of the meeting to explain why the normal protocol is not being followed, and ensure everybody that they can do their updates the next time, people will be more willing to engage in the work at hand.

4) Meetings to share information should be relevant to every attendee.

When sharing information with a broad range of people, the impact is greater if the information is equally relevant to all of the attendees. If there is a topic of interest or concern to only a few people, a separate meeting should be scheduled or another communication medium should be chosen. The attendees who have no interest in that item will see the discussion as a waste of time and will have difficulty in being engaged in the other topics.

On the other hand, establishing a consistent commitment to relevance will have positive impacts in many areas of meeting management. If you know that you are invited for a reason (Tip #2) and that the major discussions will concern you in some way, you will be a lot less likely to have to consume two liters of coffee before attending in order to stay awake for long stretches of irrelevant information sharing.

5) Meetings to understand complex issues should have participants representing a variety of backgrounds.

In order to fully explore the possibilities of issues with multiple dimensions, it is important to have diverse people in the meeting. Often, an issue is hard to completely understand because all of those looking at the issue have similar backgrounds and viewpoints. A more diverse meeting can be extremely valuable in terms of the quality of the solutions and understanding mutually created.

Actually, one of the primary purposes of a meeting in the first place is to share ideas. If there are eight participants with the same background, experience, personality and knowledge, then seven of those people are irrelevant. Identify the key dimensions of the issue from the beginning, and find participants with those backgrounds and interests to engage in the conversation.

6) Meetings to solve a problem should have participants who have a mutual interest in the solution.

Everybody involved in the creation and execution of the actions that follow a problem resolution discussion should have equally important reasons for wanting the solution to succeed. If there are participants who do not have a vested interest in the solution, they will tend to offer whatever opinion occurs to them in the moment, regardless of the effectiveness of their opinion. It is best to keep the discussion amongst those who will be impacted.

There are times when you feel you should invite some people who may not be directly impacted by the solution but should be greatly informed as to the outcome. While this seems expeditious, it is better to schedule additional meetings for the purpose of information-sharing.

7) "Official" meetings are dictated by law or organizational by-laws.

Formal meetings that are governed either by charter or by law should be conducted by guidelines such as "Robert's Rules of Order." This approach is actually less about effectiveness and efficiency than it is about thoroughness and protocol. The criteria and purpose for these meetings should be documented as well in some formal description.

On the other hand, we all need protection from the person who was a 6th-grade parliamentarian and insists on a rigid process for discussion. In a non-official setting it can actually be counter-productive to insist on "Robert's Rules of Order." It is more effective when group members agree on how they will manage a meeting than when they fanatically address a set of arbitrary rules when they are not called for.

FORMING AN AGENDA

"When the outcome of a meeting is another meeting, it has been a lousy meeting." Herbert Hoover

8) Create a process for determining agenda items.

One of the great time wasters of meetings is in having an inadequate or non-existent agenda. If there is no clear agreement on how items should be submitted, meetings will be longer and less organized than necessary because of the multitude of spontaneous topics that arise. Items should either be submitted by a specific time to a specific person, or decided by the group leader. However you collect these topics, the important thing is to have a uniform understanding of the process by all attendees.

If you do not insist on an agenda, you are undermining the impact of your meeting and increasing the level of frustration for everybody who participates.

9) Require the topic, the desired outcome, and the time needed for all agenda item submissions.

If you are the lucky person who receives agenda items for the meeting, you will sometimes be challenged to determine exactly what the purpose of the item is supposed to be or how long it should take to cover the topic. The person who submits the item will be the one who is most clear on what he or she expects to have happen.

An agenda item where the presenter is simply sharing information should be planned into the meeting differently than an agenda item where a discussion and decision are to take place (more on this later). All of the information about the reason for the topic and time needed should be available when the agenda is planned... This information included with the agenda will also allow your participants to better prepare

10) Highlight the start time and stop time on the agenda.

It is important to provide a visible facilitation tool within the agenda to help keep the meeting on track and within the scheduled time period. While this seems like small tip, it emphasizes the fact that the meeting will exist within a defined period. Remember that time management is not just an organizational tool. It is representative of your respect of the meeting topics and the participants. Even if this is a standing meeting, it is important to have this visual reminder in front of attendees.

Make this as easy as possible for yourself. If you are most comfortable saying "2:00-2:15 Review of Finance Report" then do it. If you would rather format the agenda as "15 Minutes – Review of Finance Report," that works as well. (Although no Finance Report has ever been given in fifteen minutes!)

11) Assess the participant's schedules when organizing the agenda to accommodate legitimate time conflicts.

This tip is difficult for many to adopt because of the strong sense that everybody should start the meeting and end the meeting together. While this approach is certainly easier to manage, it is also important to consider the other priorities for each individual. To make your meetings more effective, you need to engage the right people at the right time.

If you need an expert to participate in a complex discussion, but you need three other members for a discussion on strategic planning, schedule the agenda to allow the expert to come for or leave after the discussion on the topic relevant to him or her. People will appreciate the respect for their time and be more inclined to give 100% of their focus to the task when they are present.

12) Show the topic, time allotment, activity and sponsor for each item on the agenda

To most people, it is obvious that a meeting agenda should show each topic and the time allotted for discussion. To get the most engagement from your participants, it is also important to show the activity or result that is expected from the discussion and the person who is responsible for leading that part of the meeting.

Such detail not only allows everybody to see what kind of task they have ahead, but it visually represents the multiple responsibilities for making the meeting a success. This approach reinforces a sense of ownership since the documentation will be clear for anybody wanting to review it in the future.

13) Include the list of invitees on the agenda so others can see who will be in attendance.

The agenda should not only serve as a preparation tool and a guide during the meeting, but as a document of who was involved in each discussion. By indicating who will be in attendance at a meeting, participants can get a feel for the overall nature of the discussion, the importance of the topic, etc. Like many of the other suggestions, this one depends on getting the agenda to participants before the meeting (see Tip #1).

By providing the list of expected attendees, others participating in the meeting will have an opportunity to ensure key people are scheduled to attend. Otherwise, it may not be obvious until it is too late that one or two individuals were overlooked in the process of arranging the meeting.

14) Plan a break time into the agenda if the meeting will exceed ninety minutes.

In some meeting cultures, there seems to be a belief that participants should not take breaks if the meeting is truly important to them. This is a common and counterproductive approach. Regardless of the importance of the topic, it is unrealistic to expect everybody to stay engaged in a meeting without the opportunity for occasional breaks. In fact, reasonable breaks ensure that the important topics in the meeting have the full attention of the participants.

This is not only a biological issue but a psychological one as well. For attendees to stay mentally engaged, they need to occasionally rest their attention and allow their minds to reflect on the conversation at hand. It is not uncommon that the end of a break also signals a new approach to a conflict or a new idea in the conversation.

15) Include "Review of Meeting" as the last five minutes of every agenda.

This may be one of the easiest and most immediately rewarding tips in this book. If you follow up with participants a week, a day or even a few hours after the meeting, you may get helpful insights into improving future meetings, but the attention of the participants will have gone to other things. If you ask people how they felt about the meeting before they actually leave the room, you will find that there are ideas in the moment that otherwise would not be shared.

If this item is approached with a spirit of continuous improvement, the feedback will be relevant and can be considered as an opportunity to make useful adjustments to future meetings. This also keeps post-meeting complaints (whining) to a minimum because people can express their opinions before they leave.

16) Arrange the agenda in a sequence to best fit the purpose of the meeting.

Agenda items are often added to a meeting in the order in which they are received. As a result, the earlier items will have more focus as a matter of default rather than as a result of strategically examining the agenda. While this may be one way to encourage people to submit their agenda items early (first come, first served), it might not be the most effective way to manage the conversation.

As you will see with the next few tips, there are different ways to sequence a meeting for maximum results. Agenda items should be structured to the character and objectives desired for each specific meeting. Even if you are participating in a standing meeting, each session should be organized in the manner most effective to the outcomes.

17) Sequence the agenda items from least- to most-important if participants need to "ease into" the topic or if some participants will arrive late.

There are two practical reasons to start with the "easy" topics in a meeting. First, it might be that some participants will have only a short period of time between the meeting and a prior commitment or have some other legitimate reason why they are going to be late. The meeting agenda should then be arranged so the least important topics (or the topics directly involving the least number of participants) are first.

A second appropriate situation for this arrangement of topics is when a specific issue in the agenda is going to engage not only the mind but the emotions of the participants. If there is a topic likely to cause conflict or to have a great impact on the meeting attendees, it should be dealt with after covering more mundane issues.

18) Sequence the agenda from most- to least-important if you want to ensure time and energy on a priority issue.

In a similar vein to Tip #17, participants will have a finite amount of attention and energy to spend at a meeting. If there is a crucial issue that must be concluded during the meeting it might be necessary to simply dispense with the more routine matters for a later discussion and get right to the main topic.

As hard as it is to actually do this, there are times when a meeting should truly have only one agenda item so that people can focus their entire energy on it. If there are multiple items, but one is much more important than the others, a focus on this item first will allow for possible flexibility in the agenda. This flexibility leads us to the next tip.

19) Never trade meeting effectiveness for rigid agenda control.

It is possible that any given meeting will develop in a way where additional time should be given to a specific topic. At other times a new but crucial topic may come up during the meeting. This is one of the reasons participants will sometimes argue against the use of an agenda. This assumes that you either have no structure or a rigid, inflexible one.

The key to making this tip work is to *openly discuss* any changes to an agenda with participants in the meeting. If it appears that the agenda needs to be changed "in the moment," pause and review the potential changes with everybody in attendance. Make notes on the written copies of the agenda as to the changes and get agreement that this is in line with the opinions of the participants. Once you have changed the agenda, you are able to focus on the topic at hand.

20) Provide each participant with a final copy of the agenda twenty four hours prior to the meeting.

Each attendee to the meeting should have their own copy of the agenda at least a day in advance of coming to the discussion. This allows for adequate reflection and preparation for the meeting and gives the participant the opportunity to plan the rest of their schedule in the event there have been agenda changes.

By clearly marking this document "Final Agenda" you also reinforce the idea that the plan is thought out and complete. While it is important to allow flexibility in the discussion as illustrated in Tip #19, it is also important to show that the meeting is not simply left up to chance.

By the way, it doesn't matter whether you think they will actually read it or not. If you keep make sure "Final" is final, folks will start to use it.

21) Consider displaying the agenda by flipchart or projection throughout the meeting.

A displayed agenda provides reinforcement to the meeting plan. It is also easier for the meeting facilitator or leader to reference the progress of the meeting if it is posted in a prominent position in the room for all to see.

An additional advantage to having a posted copy of the agenda is that any changes that need to be made to the agenda can easily be noted and agreed upon by the entire meeting body. This eliminates further confusion if changes are made.

If the agenda is posted on a flipchart during the review of the meeting, there is the added benefit of providing the leader with an easy map of the meeting for review (see Tip #44) to see if participants felt each topic, timing and discussion was valuable.

BEFORE THE MEETING BEGINS

"Any simple problem can be made unsolvable if enough meetings are held to discuss it" Unknown

22) Consider the one or two participants that must be at the meeting and start scheduling with their calendars.

It is most likely that there are one or two participants that especially need to be in the discussion due to their experience, involvement with the topic, or the impact of their role on the outcome. By starting the scheduling process with their calendars, you can avoid a lot of negotiations and the waste of time associated with holding a meeting without the right players involved.

This is another case where each meeting may be organized differently. However, the increase in effectiveness offsets the extra effort and potential extra meetings.

23) Avoid scheduling Monday morning / Friday afternoon meetings if possible.

Standing meetings are often scheduled for either first thing Monday morning or last thing Friday afternoon. While this cruel practice is generally to ensure maximum availability, it might be that this schedule also inherently detracts from the effectiveness of your meeting.

Allowing people at least an hour or so on Monday morning to get themselves into a non-weekend mindset is not only respectful but also most productive. Friday afternoon meetings are disliked for many reasons, sometimes just because it is Friday.

Sometimes the issue is fatigue and lack of energy at the end of the week. It is also reasonable to allow people their individual time to wrap up issues that need to be closed before the weekend or to prepare for the week ahead.

24) Check organizational calendars to see if there are larger events that may conflict with your meetings.

It is easy to forget that other people have additional responsibilities or engagements at a time where you are focused on the purpose and outcomes of your meeting. As part of any organization, large or small, you will be subject to the events and schedules that will affect your participants. Holidays, town hall meetings or other events should be taken into account to avoid the frustration of having to reschedule and to avoid confusing your participants about which priority they should hold.

If the meeting is a large one, a long one, or of crucial importance, it is worth considering local events in your planning as well. Sports tournaments or long awaited concerts can cause many people to have sick grandmothers and baby-sitting responsibilities.

25) Invite the right people.

Consider the following:

a) Who needs the information discussed at this meeting?
b) Who has the information necessary for the discussion?
c) Who is affected by the issue?
d) Who can help resolve the issue?
e) Who needs to be involved now in preparation of later participation?
f) Who needs to be involved now for political reason?

Nobody should be invited for the sole reason that they are curious and want to attend. As stated in earlier tips, each participant should have a clear personal or professional reason to be involved for truly high impact.

26) Consider the level and authority of those you invite.

There are practical reasons to consider the mix of authority that you invite to a meeting. Employees have a different perspective on issues than executives or managers have, because of the point of view of day-to-day responsibility and scope. Having all perspectives in the discussion can add an outstanding quality to our discussion, but only if all attendees can participate equally.

If you have various levels of personnel attending the same meeting, it is important to emphasize the expectation of open and honest communication. To assist with this, you should be very clear about the decision process. If there are attendees who rank higher in the organization than the decision-maker on the issue, it is especially important to clarify the roles and responsibilities with everybody prior to the start of the meeting.

27) Invite larger numbers of attendees for information-sharing meetings.

If the purpose of your meeting is solely information sharing, you should invite as many people as reasonably possible. These meetings are actually more of a communication channel than a "meeting" and should be handled as such. If there is to be a question and answer period as part of the meeting, having many people in attendance will ensure that they hear not only the same message, but the same answers to the questions.

In an effort for open discussion, there is sometimes a tendency to make information-sharing meetings of a more intimate size. If you need to have open discussion about the topic because it is emotional or there are many people affected, it might be necessary to cut down on the number (see next few tips). However, if the purpose is solely to deliver news, the more people at once the better.

28) Restrict the number of attendees to problem-solving or decision-making meetings.

In a problem-solving or decision-making meeting, there may be many people who would like to hear this discussion first-hand. However, it is unrealistic to expect valuable participation in meetings of greater than 12 to 15 attendees. The optimum number seems to be closer to 8, but you may have more constituencies that need to be represented.

If you must have more than 15 in attendance, you can create a core group of 6-8 people that will actually make the decision and use the larger group for input. Let those who attend share their opinions and input and then have the final decision be made by the smaller group. Make sure that the process you chose for invitation to each session is made transparent to everybody. Everybody can then understand the purpose behind your approach.

29) Send pre-reading with the agenda.

Sending presentation material prior to the meeting allows for optimum use of your time by creating informed and prepared participants. You can dispense with much of the pre-discussion and begin with questions or clarification of the material and then focus on the matter at hand.

What do you do if attendees are not prepared? *Act as if they are.* If you have provided adequate time to review the material and everybody has had equal opportunity to do so, you should proceed with the assumption that they have read the material. If they have not completed the pre-work and you truly want to increase the effectiveness of your meeting, try adjourning and rescheduling the meeting to give everybody the opportunity to prepare. You will find very quickly that participants will take the time to study the pre-reading when they receive it before future meetings!

30) Touch base with the facilitator and key sponsors in the meeting.

Twenty-four hours before your meeting you should make sure to talk with the meeting facilitator if you have one and all of the key topic owners to ensure that they have everything they need and are prepared for the meeting. Last minute changes should be communicated in terms of attendees, topics or locations. By making sure the primary players in the meeting are all ready for the discussion, you will be able to relax a bit and prepare for the meeting yourself.

If there are necessary agenda changes that are known at the last minute, include them on the posted version of the agenda. If there is no possibility that participants can react to the change before the meeting, don't worry about sending it to everybody ahead of time. The role of the agenda is to help the process, not create useless tasks!

OFFSITE MEETINGS

"The ideal meeting is one with me as the chairman and the other members at home in bed with the flu." Lord Milverton

31) Check the equipment and seating at the location prior to the start of the meeting

On the day of the meeting, always ensure the equipment is working and the seating is as you arranged. While it may be possible to check this the day before the meeting, there are many things that can change overnight. It is best to arrange your schedule, and that of the facility personnel, to allow for a last check of all details about an hour before the meeting begins.

Some details are easy to overlook. Hotels, for example, will sometimes provide flip chart pads and stands, but no markers. Temperature of the room is another detail that can only be set on that day.

32) Prepare name tents and badges if participants may not know one another.

While this may seem to be a minor detail, it is very helpful for an effective meeting if people know the person and function of a participant during the discussion. Even doing introductions around the table(s) will not suffice as all of this information is shared at one time and much of it will be forgotten.

A simple name tag on a lanyard will also work better than a pin or clasp type of name tag since it does not damage clothing. Ideally, the name should be printed on both sides of the name tag since lanyards are notorious for flipping over just at the moment the person begins to speak.

Encourage attendees to use the badges and tents for every day of the offsite event. It is a courtesy to everybody in the meeting and encourages much easier conversation both during and after the session.

33) Provide logistic and contact information at least one week in advance for all meeting participants.

You can eliminate a lot of extra telephone calls and emails if you can provide logistic information to all participants at least a week in advance of the meeting. This should include location, address, lodging (if appropriate), contact telephone numbers, food arrangements, dress code, and any other information you think might be helpful.

If people are staying the night at the location, you should have this information to them three weeks in advance with additional data about the hotel, expenses and how reservations should be made. If they are on their own, most people appreciate a list of recommendations which allows them to focus less on the logistics and more on the reasons why they are there.

34) Order fruit and other health snacks rather than cookies or brownies during breaks.

While this tip may sound like a matter of taste, there is a practical reason for providing snacks along the lines of vegetables and fruits rather than sweets. While they are healthier choices, fruits, nuts and other snacks will also offset the energy slumps that normally occur when an individual's blood sugar goes up with the snack and then drops within a short period afterward. Considering that a long meeting challenges alertness by sheer exhaustion, any small thing you can do to help avoid major drops in energy will add to your meeting effectiveness.

The same consideration should be made for beverages as well. Natural fruit juice and bottled water are important to have along with the sodas. Tea is also a nice addition. If you ever invite *me* to attend one of your meetings, coffee and cookies will do fine, thank you.

35) Secure offsite contact numbers.

To balance the need for contact with the need for focused and uninterrupted participation, arrange with the offsite location to have messages relayed from telephone or fax. Most people are not intentionally rude but are caught between priorities if they receive a call from a family member or the office during your meeting. By having those calls come through an offsite number, you can better manage the flow of interruptions during the discussion.

Make sure to inform your meeting participants on the process of handling calls and messages. The best bet is having a business center collect messages for retrieval during the breaks. Next best choice is to have a board or table *outside of the room* where people can check. It is most disruptive to have messages delivered into the meeting and handed to the participant. Interrupting the session should only be in the case of an urgent situation.

DURING THE MEETING
"Even if you're on the right track, you'll get run over if you sit there." Will Rogers

36) Start the meeting with energy and enthusiasm.
The first few minutes of any meeting will set the tone for the rest of the discussion. Make sure to begin with the positive, e.g. what will be the results when the meeting is successful. Providing negative input at the beginning, or rattling off mundane items before getting started will serve to depress the energy in the room. Even if it will be a difficult meeting, focus on the value of the meeting to give the session a positive session.

"Before we get started…" should be avoided at all costs. Once you start, you start. Include details and logistics as an agenda item after the welcome and beginning of the meeting. Your participants might actually remember them that way as well.

37) Use the appropriate introduction process for adults and professional attendees.

Clever ice breakers or silly sorts of introduction exercises are ineffective and often insulting to adult attendees. This is not to insult those of you who love to have ice-breaking games. These activities are best if it is a training session rather than a meeting. They may also work if the meeting is an offsite event of a full day or more. However, if it is a meeting with a professional focus, the introductions at the beginning should be professional as well.

While some may argue that starting with a clever ice-breaker sets a positive energetic tone for the meeting, it only does so for those who are comfortable with these types of exercises. Those who are more reticent or simply uncomfortable in groups of new people will not be thrilled or energized by the activity. I know they have told you they were in the past, but they hated it. ☺

38) Start the meeting with a review of the agenda.

Ensure all participants understand the objectives of the meeting by reviewing the agenda items, objectives and sponsor at the start of the session. Attendees should have an opportunity to ask questions or comment on the overall structure before beginning the meeting. This allows everybody to start with the same understanding and agreement and allows you to focus on the content rather than the possibility that a surprise topic is going to arise.

The challenge with some meetings at this point is the feeling that they are wasting time and not getting into the heart of the discussion. This is a place where you should hold your ground. The agenda of the meeting should be a consensus decision before getting underway. This allows the entire group to be accountable for the topics discussed and any decisions made along the way that might influence the agreed upon time commitment.

39) Consider additions to the agenda carefully.

People will sometimes suggest that additional items be added to the discussion. Be very cautious about doing this. First, it may undermine your attempt at creating high-impact meetings because it is unlikely that attendees will have the same opportunity to prepare for these new items as they have for the ones planned on the agenda.

Second, you will need to consider the consequence to the planned meeting when you are adding new items. Each sponsor of an agenda item has already provided an estimate of time needed and the objective of the item. If you add new topics, you will have to eliminate some time from somebody's topic or add time to the meeting. This impacts everybody's ability to plan and detracts from the impact of the meeting. Everybody in the meeting should be aware of these consequences.

40) Provide a "parking lot."

The good news is that an enthusiastic and engaged conversation tends to be more creative and provoke more thinking. The bad news is that the additional creativity and thinking may also provoke more potential topics to discuss. Not all of these will be relevant *for the moment*, but many will be ideas that you don't want to just dismiss.

A "parking lot" is a flipchart or notepad where a list of items is kept that need to be addressed in a future meeting. This allows participants to bring up issues as they think of them but will not force the meeting into discussions on unrelated or less important topics. When the conversation takes off down a tangent that is not relevant to the flow of the current meeting, simply asking "Can we put this in the parking lot for later" will allow you to capture it, but move on with the topic at hand.

41) Appoint roles for the meeting.

Choose a time keeper and note recorder at the beginning of the meeting if none is permanently appointed. If there is no third-party facilitator for the meeting, appoint somebody to keep the meeting on track. Ideally, these appointments should be made prior to the start of the meeting, but if necessary you can do this at the beginning.

These roles may seem nominal, but they are important to the process of the meeting. If everybody is watching the time and making the notes, then too many people are devoting energy to administrative tasks. Since those in attendance also want to participate, make sure to separate the tasks, e.g. one person watching the time and flow of the agenda while another person is taking the notes.

CLOSING AND FOLLOWING UP
"The prayer of the chicken hawk does not get him the chicken."
Swahili Proverb

42) Summarize the agreements and actions decided during the meeting.

By the end of the meeting there may be numerous agreements and actions decided upon. It is important to summarize these before officially closing the meeting to ensure that everybody is clear on what has happened during the meeting. This allows you to be confident that nobody will feel (or say) later they did not understand what had happened.

The summary of agreements and actions gives all meeting participants confirmation that the important points have been documented. If there is some disagreement, but the meeting has come to a close, you can also agree that any of the topics may need to be revisited in the next meeting.

43) Schedule the next meeting.

The best time to schedule the next meeting is at the end of the meeting you are in. If you are participating in a regularly scheduled meeting it is a good time to confirm that the next meeting will be held as planned or that it is not necessary.

While scheduling the meeting, make a quick review of the parking lot items to be addressed next time. If there are open questions about who should be invited, these can (and should) all be covered at the end as you are scheduling.

One bonus tip. People have a tendency to start "checking out" as you start to close up the meeting. Encourage them to give the meeting a few more minutes of their attention. The payoff is that hours (or even days) of chasing details can be offset by simply hitting some of the points before they leave.

44) Evaluate the meeting.

The only time you can get an accurate evaluation of the meeting is before attendees have departed. Sending a follow-up evaluation is less effective and usually not worth the effort. Your evaluation should cover areas such as the relevance of the topics, the facility and logistics, the manner in which the meeting was conducted, and any ideas for future improvement.

This evaluation doesn't need to be pseudo-scientific. Asking "what did we do well today" and "what should we improve" may be the only questions you need.

For this discussion to be helpful, make sure that it's not all about logistics. "The lights could have been brighter" is an important feedback, but the best input is at an effectiveness level. What could have been done to make the meeting more worthwhile?

45) Distribute the notes promptly.

Ideally, participants should receive the minutes and other notes from the meeting within 24 hours of completion. While this is not always realistic, the follow-up information should be distributed within three to four days at the maximum. This is a good time frame as a reminder of the meeting and ensures that the discussion is still fresh enough in the minds of the attendees to recall the meaning behind the notes.

These notes can be e-mailed or distributed through hardcopy and should include a note thanking the participant for their involvement in the meeting. If there were any ancillary materials that were to be sent to participants afterwards they should be included at the same time.

46) Debrief the meeting.

As soon as possible after the meeting you should debrief with the others who were involved in the set-up. You can cover the notes from the meeting evaluation as well as discuss any of your observations that may not have come up in the evaluation but that you realize could be improved. You should make sure in this discussion that you identify the parts of the meeting that went very well and especially those portions of the discussion that showed marked improvement. These are the areas from which you can build in future meetings.

If you were the only person responsible for making the meeting happen, you should identify one person from the participant list with whom you have a relationship and have this discussion with them. While you may agree with the points that came from Tip #45, you will have a bigger picture perspective as well and should think about the overall experience.

NOW, STOP WASTING YOUR TIME!!

You would think that you could simply offer other people the opportunity to make their time more effective by following a few of these tips and they would jump at the change. You will discover, however, that the greatest challenge to creating high-impact meetings is the resistance to change that participants in the meeting will typically have.

On the final pages is a list of the 46 meeting tips. Look through them again and decide which area would give you the greatest impact if you were to change it at the next meeting. Most importantly, make a commitment to continue through the resistance of change until participants see the value of the direction you are going with your meeting. Don't worry about getting everybody to agree with everything at once. Making incremental changes with visible results will convince even the toughest skeptic over time.

MEETING CHECKLIST

1. Inform all participants on the purpose of the meeting and why they are there.

2. Cancel the meeting if there is no agenda within 24 hours of the meeting.

3. Limit the topics on the agenda, especially if the meeting is to generate ideas.

4. Make information-sharing relevant to every participant.

5. Invite attendees with the right expertise and background.

6. Ensure all participants have a vested interest in developing solutions.

7. Use "rules-of-order" for official meetings.

8. Create a process for determining agenda items.

9. Require the topic, the desired outcome, and the time needed (including discussion) for all agenda item submissions.

10. Highlight the start time and stop time on the agenda.

11. Assess the participant's schedules when organizing the agenda to accommodate legitimate time conflicts.

12. Show the topic, time allotment, activity and sponsor for each item on the agenda

13. Include the list of invitees on the agenda so others can see who will be in attendance.

14. Plan a break time into the agenda if the meeting will exceed ninety minutes.

15. Include "Review of Meeting" as the last five minutes of every agenda.

16. Arrange the agenda in a sequence to best fit the purpose of the meeting.

17. Sequence the agenda from least- to most-important items if participants need to "ease into" the topic or there is the likelihood that some participants will arrive late.

18. Sequence the agenda from most- to least-important if you want to ensure time and energy on a priority issue.

19. Never trade meeting effectiveness for rigid agenda control.

20. Provide each participant with a final copy of the agenda twenty four hours prior to the meeting.

21. Consider displaying the agenda by flipchart or projection throughout the meeting.

22. Consider the one or two participants that must be at the meeting and start scheduling with their calendars.

23. Avoid scheduling Monday morning / Friday afternoon meetings if possible.

24. Check organizational calendars to see if there are larger events that may conflict with your meetings.

25. Invite the right people.

26. Consider the level and authority of those you invite.

27. Invite larger numbers of attendees for information-sharing meetings.

28. Restrict the number of attendees to problem-solving or decision-making meetings.

29. Send pre-reading with the agenda.

30. Touch base with the facilitator and key sponsors in the meeting.

31. Check the equipment and seating at the location prior to the start of the meeting

32. Prepare name tents and badges if participants may not know one another.

33. Provide logistic and contact information at least one week in advance for all meeting participants.

34. Order fruit and other health snacks rather than cookies or brownies during breaks.

35. Secure offsite contact numbers.

36. Start the meeting with energy and enthusiasm.

37. Use the appropriate introduction process for adults and professional attendees.

38. Start the meeting with a review of the agenda.

39. Consider additions to the agenda carefully.

40. Provide a "parking lot."

41. Appoint roles for the meeting.

42. Summarize the agreements and actions decided during the meeting.

43. Schedule the next meeting.

44. Evaluate the meeting.

45. Distribute the notes promptly.

46. Debrief the meeting.

Dr. Todd Thomas is a speaker, author, educator and coach who has worked with leaders from around the world over the last two decades. He is an Associate Professor at the DeVos Graduate School of Management and lives in Michigan with his wife, Karen, and two children, Emily and Bryce. You can follow his blog at http://www.DrToddThomas.com or connect with him at:

Twitter: http://twitter.com/DrTodd2010

Facebook: http://facebook.com/drtoddthomas

LinkedIn: http://www.linkedin.com/in/drtodd

High Impact Meetings: A Guide for Greater Productivity can be customized for your organization or customers by adding your logo or message to the inside front and back pages. Discounts on volume purchases are also available. Please contact Dr. Todd for more information.

www.ingramcontent.com/pod-product-compliance
Lightning Source LLC
Chambersburg PA
CBHW061521180526
45171CB00001B/271